Communication
Skills Profile

Communication Skills Profile

ELENA TOSCA

Jossey-Bass
Pfeiffer

San Francisco

Published by

Jossey-Bass
Pfeiffer

350 Sansome Street, 5th Floor
San Francisco, California 94104-1342
(415) 433-1740; Fax (415) 433-0499
(800) 274-4434; Fax (800) 569-0443

Visit our website at: www.pfeiffer.com

Printing   10   9   8   7   6   5   4   3

CONTENTS

Elena Tosca is a partner with Akron, a team of consultants, executive trainers, and speakers who offer consulting and educational services to help people in organizations to achieve better performance. The team works to expand the field of organizational learning, systems thinking, dialogue, and mental models.

Ms. Tosca specializes in people management, dialogue, mental models, team learning and development, systems thinking, and organizational learning. She successfully designs, develops, and conducts training interventions throughout Italy and Europe, using a practical "hands-on" approach.

Her clients include large and small organizations in various fields, such as IBM, Heineken, W. L. Gore & Associates, Glaxo Wellcome, Fox-Bompani, Procond Elettronica, SIFI, Colmark, Eniricerche, and Regione Marche.

She is a member of the board of directors of the Italian Society of System Dymamics and serves on the editorial advisory board of the professional journal *Systems Thinking in Action*, which is published by the Italian Society of System Dynamics.

Ms. Tosca is a coauthor, with Tommaso Bertani and Vittorio D'Amato, of the book *Come costruire il futuro dell'impresa*, published by F. Angeli in 1994.

CHAPTER 1

The Questionnaire

Communication is essential to organizational success. Effective communication helps to develop interpersonal understanding and enhances a person's ability to solve problems, whether at home or at work. Work teams, in particular, need people who can communicate effectively.

Despite this need, communication inside and outside of organizations is often ineffective. Two difficulties are involved: sharing information and finding common ground.

The Communication Skills Profile was designed to help people who want to gain a thorough knowledge of the processes of communication and to improve their effectiveness as communicators.

The chapters in the profile are organized in a specific sequence for most effective learning. It is recommended that respondents read each chapter and do the activities in the order suggested, as follows:

Chapter 1. Forty-eight questions designed to enable individuals to assess the effectiveness of their own communications

Chapter 2. Brief descriptions of the bases of communication and dialogue

Chapter 3. Predictions of individual results

Chapter 4. Scoring and creation of individual profiles

Chapter 5. Interpretation and analysis

Chapter 6. Development of action plans

Chapter 7. Feedback and processing

Chapter 8. Notes for work groups

The Communication Skills Profile

Instructions: Each of the following six sections consists of eight statements. For each statement, select your response from the following scale and write the number in the blank to the left of the statement. Do not total your scores at this point.

If the statement is *nearly always* true for you, choose "6."

If the statement is *often* true for you, choose "5."

If the statement is *sometimes* true for you, choose "4."

If the statement is *not often* true for you, choose "3."

If the statement is *rarely* true for you, choose "2."

If the statement is *never* true for you, choose "1."

If the statement is *nearly always* true for you, choose "6."

If the statement is *often* true for you, choose "5."

If the statement is *sometimes* true for you, choose "4."

If the statement is *not often* true for you, choose "3."

If the statement is *rarely* true for you, choose "2."

If the statement is *never* true for you, choose "1."

Section A: Slowing My Thought Processes

_____ 1. I understand how I make decisions.

_____ 2. I look for alternate interpretations of the data at my disposal.

_____ 3. I am aware of how my interpretations determine my choice of action.

_____ 4. I explicitly examine all courses of action that are possible and coherent with my interpretation.

_____ 5. In new situations, I identify the factors that make a first impression.

_____ 6. I show how these factors influence my behavior.

_____ 7. I am aware of the underlying convictions at the basis of my interpretations.

_____ 8. I check how my interpretation of these factors fits with my previous convictions.

_____ **Total Score**

_____ **Average Score** (Total Score ÷ 8)

If the statement is *nearly always* true for you, choose "6."

If the statement is *often* true for you, choose "5."

If the statement is *sometimes* true for you, choose "4."

If the statement is *not often* true for you, choose "3."

If the statement is *rarely* true for you, choose "2."

If the statement is *never* true for you, choose "1."

Section B: Making Myself Understood

_____ 9. I use a form of language my partner understands.

_____ 10. I check to be sure that both my partner and I attribute the same meaning to the terms and expressions I use.

_____ 11. I explain the entire process by which I formed a certain opinion.

_____ 12. I present the data that support my idea in clear and comprehensible ways.

_____ 13. When I present data, I eliminate what seems superfluous and explain why, but I retain the data for my partner in case he or she should need them.

_____ 14. I use examples that explain my position and its consequences.

_____ 15. I use metaphors and examples to make what I say clearer.

_____ 16. I use comparisons that are familiar to my partner.

_____ **Total Score**

_____ **Average Score** (Total Score ÷ 8)

If the statement is *nearly always* true for you, choose "6."

If the statement is *often* true for you, choose "5."

If the statement is *sometimes* true for you, choose "4."

If the statement is *not often* true for you, choose "3."

If the statement is *rarely* true for you, choose "2."

If the statement is *never* true for you, choose "1."

Section C: Testing My Conclusions

_____ 17. I clearly separate data from opinions.

_____ 18. I promote analysis and inquiry to verify my ideas and my interpretation of facts.

_____ 19. I check any data that are in contrast with my opinion, doing my utmost to understand their meaning and how they might influence my conclusions.

_____ 20. I clearly indicate weak points in my reasoning in order to try to overcome them together with my partner.

_____ 21. I allow others to ask for further explanations about my ideas and opinions.

_____ 22. When someone challenges my point of view, I make sure I do not consider it a personal attack.

_____ 23. I accept criticism as a way of improving.

_____ 24. I think it is important that others understand my point of view so that they can give me their opinions clearly and explicitly.

_____ **Total Score**

_____ **Average Score** (Total Score ÷ 8)

If the statement is *nearly always* true for you, choose "6."

If the statement is *often* true for you, choose "5."

If the statement is *sometimes* true for you, choose "4."

If the statement is *not often* true for you, choose "3."

If the statement is *rarely* true for you, choose "2."

If the statement is *never* true for you, choose "1."

Section D: Listening Constructively

_____ 25. I am aware of the difference between "hearing" and "listening to" my partner.

_____ 26. I do my utmost to listen with care to my partner, concentrating on what is happening.

_____ 27. I concentrate on the content of what is being said.

_____ 28. I take quick notes on the most important things, making sure I do not get distracted by notes that are too detailed.

_____ 29. If I don't have time to listen or have other thoughts on my mind, I make sure that I don't merely pretend to listen but postpone the conversation to a more appropriate time.

_____ 30. When I speak to someone, I make sure I eliminate all possible sources of distraction.

_____ 31. I try to read body language in order to understand my partner better.

_____ 32. I avoid formulating an answer in my head while my partner is still speaking.

_____ **Total Score**

_____ **Average Score** (Total Score ÷ 8)

If the statement is *nearly always* true for you, choose "6."

If the statement is *often* true for you, choose "5."

If the statement is *sometimes* true for you, choose "4."

If the statement is *not often* true for you, choose "3."

If the statement is *rarely* true for you, choose "2."

If the statement is *never* true for you, choose "1."

Section E: Getting to the Essence

_____ 33. I make sure I have understood my partner and tell him or her that this is important for me.

_____ 34. I ask questions aimed at understanding better.

_____ 35. When I ask for clarification, I do so in a clear, unaggressive manner.

_____ 36. I make sure not to blame my partner if I do not understand what he or she has said.

_____ 37. I try to identify the areas I have not understood in order to ask simple, clear questions.

_____ 38. If I think it necessary, I take time to think things over, postponing the rest of the conversation to a more appropriate time.

_____ 39. If my partner asks, I give him or her the time to gather all the data needed to support his or her opinion.

_____ 40. I try to help my partner make his or her thought processes clear so I can understand how he or she reached certain conclusions.

_____ **Total Score**

_____ **Average Score** (Total Score ÷ 8)

If the statement is *nearly always* true for you, choose "6."

If the statement is *often* true for you, choose "5."

If the statement is *sometimes* true for you, choose "4."

If the statement is *not often* true for you, choose "3."

If the statement is *rarely* true for you, choose "2."

If the statement is *never* true for you, choose "1."

Section F: Exploring Disagreement

_____ 41. I try to find the cause of a disagreement in order to understand its origins.

_____ 42. I use techniques aimed at clarifying disagreements in order to reduce conflict and embarrassment.

_____ 43. I am convinced that disagreement is an important source of learning for all members of the group.

_____ 44. If the conversation with my partner comes to a standstill, I look for help from a third party who may have another point of view.

_____ 45. I make explicit the points of agreement and disagreement in order to guide discussion.

_____ 46. I ensure that I am not led by emotions and encourage others not to be.

_____ 47. I encourage the people around me to analyze and explore disagreements.

_____ 48. If I realize that I am in a situation of conflict and difference of opinion, I say so explicitly rather than hiding what I think.

_____ **Total Score**

_____ **Average Score** (Total Score ÷ 8)

CHAPTER 2

The Bases
of Communication
and Dialogue

We live in what has rightly been called the information era: We all have access to a far greater volume of information than was the case just a few years ago. Publications, mass media, and the information superhighway are integral parts of our day-to-day lives. It is hardly surprising that at times we feel a little disoriented.

Could we also define our era as the Communication Age? In terms of the sheer number of messages that are sent around the world, the reply would certainly be yes. However, communications cannot be measured merely by counting the number of bottles thrown into the sea; it is far more difficult to ascertain how many of these bottles are picked up, how many messages are read, and how each is understood. In other words, communication involves at least two people, a code, and a decode.

And yet in today's world, we seem so busy launching messages that we hardly have time to verify how well any of them reach their destinations. Similarly, we tend barely to listen to the messages that do arrive; at most we hear them, without challenging what they really mean.

Technology encourages us to replace the verb "communicate" with verbs like "transmit", "broadcast," or "launch"—all words that pay insufficient attention to the receivers of our messages.

Think about books and courses on communication: What do they generally teach? Answers might include how to express yourself clearly, which words to use and which to avoid, what kind of tone to adopt, and how to be convincing or persuasive. Very little time is dedicated to verifying seriously and honestly what the listeners have actually understood. And even less time is spent on listening skills.

All the emphasis appears to be on "transmission." Although transmission is an important part of communication, it is only a part. This is true both of the media and of face-to-face meetings. It is true of families and the relations between parents and children, of organizations and the relations between colleagues who know little about each other and understand each other even less. Too often people end up watching TV or going to the movies rather than talking to people.

This impoverishes life, and clearly there is a great deal of room for improvement. The first step is to understand the importance of communication in a profound sense. Subsequently it will be possible to analyze the processes of communication more thoroughly and to learn how to master these processes.

The Importance of Communication

During the Middle Ages, a single individual, such as Galileo, could master practically all known human knowledge, being a mathematician, architect, and anatomist who made rapid connections between different disciplines. Subsequently science developed so rapidly that it was no longer possible for an individual to master so many areas of investigation. The world became specialized, starting in school, where children were assessed on individual performance, which encouraged them to work alone and to try to solve problems alone. Physicists were physicists, doctors doctors, and teachers teachers.

Now, however, problems can no longer be solved by following the direction of specialization and fragmentation. The world has become so complex that no physicist, doctor, or teacher has anything but a tiny view of it. No single individual can hope to achieve the degree of knowledge required to solve complex problems. Organizations, especially, do not work like this. Communication among individuals is vital. Groups of people with a broad range of skills can solve problems, provided that they are able to pool their resources.

Not long ago, individuals with particularly strong personalities and a high degree of competence in one specific area could start businesses and turn them into hugely successful organizations. That era is over. Now we all depend on one another; we work in groups, live in groups, and prosper only as groups.

In the future, individuals will be successful only if they know how to communicate with others. They will have good interpersonal relations with colleagues and will obtain excellent results at work. Their communication skills will enable them to understand their colleagues and to tap their potential. These individuals will work in a communication continuum, alongside others, not in isolation. They will learn from others and enable others to learn from them.

Similarly, successful organizations will be the ones best able to bring different experiences together and to foster an atmosphere of genuine communication and interchange. Individuals will be like the pieces of a puzzle, incapable on their own of solving complex problems but vital as parts of the whole.

To that end, we have to relearn communication skills, the ability to express ourselves clearly and frankly and to listen to others who do the same. The results will not be disappointing, either in private life or at work.

The Process of Communication

Communication is the process by which an individual (a source) communicates with another individual (a receiver). It is a highly complex process in which a number of different elements influence the effectiveness of the communication.

Two fundamental aspects of the communication process are the *coding* and *decoding*. Whoever wants to communicate a message chooses a code believed to be understandable to his or her partner. The partner decodes the message, believing that he or she will perfectly reproduce the contents of the message sent. Frequently this does not happen, because the message is not "clean." By this we mean two things: that the message does not contain only what was intended, and that all codes are open to a degree of subjective interpretation.

The receiver listens and selects the content of what is heard on the basis of his or her expectations; at the simplest level, this means that if we do not expect to be interested in the content of a message, we are likely to listen absentmindedly and miss a great deal of what is said. Then, if we miss most of the message, we are unlikely to be interested in it. Our impression is that our expectations have been confirmed, not that we have chosen not to listen.

At a more complex level, even if we listen with care, parts of the message will seem more interesting than others, depending on our own convictions, beliefs, and so on. We automatically classify the content of the message within our own priorities, which may not necessarily correspond to the priorities the speaker had in mind.

At another level, the message itself sets up a number of expectations. If it sounds as if the speaker is going to say a certain thing, we believe that certain thing is part of the message even if the speaker does not actually say it.

These inferences are just as important to us when we speak as when we listen. As speakers, we tend to assume that our message has been decoded properly and that our listeners have understood. As listeners, we assume that we have decoded efficiently, meaning that the speaker is really saying what we think he or she is saying. In both cases, in order to verify the effectiveness of the communication process, we need to understand these inferences and eliminate them.

A further element of inference results from the fact that all communication takes place at more than one level; in the case of verbal communication, there are what can be called a numerical element—the words themselves—and an analogical element—body language. In order to communicate effectively, these two elements should be congruous. If what we say is contradicted by body language, listeners will believe the body language. This is a vital aspect of the communication process. A relatively small part of the overall message is communicated by our words; a far higher percentage of the message is communicated more unconsciously.

The risk of communicating what we did not intend to say, or of contradicting what we actually do say, means that continuous feedback is necessary in order to verify the effectiveness of our communication.

Feedback is the only means for checking what people have understood. Essentially it means asking people to repeat our message and listening closely to what they say. We should not forget that feedback is itself a process of communication and so is similarly subject to inference.

One important feature of communication is that it is not possible not to communicate. Even if we sit in absolute silence, our silence says something about our state of mind: we are not interested, or we are bored, offended, or waiting for something important to be said.

We have only touched on some of the problems involved in communication, but these brief remarks should be enough to suggest a far greater attention to the problem than we normally give. As speakers, we should encourage people to express what they have understood; as listeners, we should give continuous feedback in order to make sure we ourselves have understood.

Dialogue

Conversation has always been an important scientific activity. A number of important discoveries have been made after virtually chance remarks because words sometimes act as catalysts.

Dialogue is a relatively new discipline that aims at creating a genuine and profound communication between individuals who think together, pooling their resources and experiences. The starting point of the discipline is the recognition that all communication has two quite distinct elements: the content of the communication (what is said) and the relationship expressed through it and created by it (how it is said).

Generally people judge the effectiveness of communication more on the basis of the second element than the first. In other words, they realize that if the relationship is going well, the content can be clarified later. However, if the relationship is going badly, then even if the content is clear, the meeting is likely to leave an impression of dissatisfaction and frustration.

Dialogue is a discipline that aims to create the right emotional climate for communication to take place effectively and efficiently. The basis for any dialogue is our willingness to get to know each other, which is expressed both by showing interest in what others have to say and by saying what we think, clearly and frankly.

Generally people tend to hide their own doubts, fears, and uncertainties. These are, however, an important part of the way people think. It is difficult to get to know someone without understanding his or her mental reservations or emotional difficulties. In nearly all cases, these remain hidden because people do not like to be judged on the basis of what they regard as their weaknesses. One of the most important elements of dialogue is the ability to listen without making judgments.

The first step is to get people to sit down together at the same table where one rule, above all, is agreed: people's words will not be judged. If the feeling is that others are trying to understand and not to come to judgment, people speak more openly and freely; they tend to communicate more effectively, too, because they do not need to use defense mechanisms.

After this initial stage, the group will be able to turn its attention to concrete problems. Without this stage, the discussions will run into obstacles that may prevent solutions from being found.

A particularly interesting thing happens in teams that have created a good atmosphere: people no longer identify themselves with their own opinions. In other words, if I criticize an opinion, it does not mean I am criticizing a person; if someone criticizes my views, I do not feel a personal attack.

The implication of this discussion is that dialogue changes the decision-making processes. The purpose of this technique is to overcome individual points of view and to reach a collective perspective capable of harnessing the experience of all the members of the group. The decisions that are reached in this way will be better than decisions reached by individuals and will reflect a common vision of the problem that all members of the group share equally.

The responsibility, therefore, is to improve individual communication skills in order to promote effective team communication, whether these teams include superiors, colleagues, or subordinates.

CHAPTER 3

Predicting
Individual Results

The two areas under evaluation in the Communication Skills Profile are (1) the ability to express one's own opinions; and (2) the ability to listen and understand others. Each area is divided into three essential skills:

1. Expressing one's own opinions includes Slowing Thought Processes, Making Yourself Understood, and Testing Your Conclusions.

2. Listening to and understanding others includes Listening Constructively, Getting to the Essence, and Exploring Disagreement.

Instructions: At this point, stop and predict your average score on the Communication Skills Profile for each of these six communication skills. Your score will be the average of your responses to the eight statements in each questionnaire section. Your predicted average scores may range from a low of "1" to a high of "6."

My Prediction

Expressing Your Own Opinions

      Section A: Slowing My Thought Processes   _____

      Section B: Making Myself Understood   _____

      Section C: Testing My Conclusions   _____

Listening and Understanding Others

      Section D: Listening Constructively   _____

      Section E: Getting to the Essence   _____

      Section F: Exploring Disagreement   _____

CHAPTER 4

Scoring the Communication Skills Profile

In this part of the Communication Skills Profile, you will compute your own scores on the questionnaire, and you will be asked to identify areas for improvement on which to base an Action Plan.

Instructions: Return to the questionnaire in the first chapter and calculate your total scores and your average scores. Transfer your average scores to the blanks in the following list.

Section A: Slowing My Thought Processes   _____

Section B: Making Myself Understood   _____

Section C: Testing My Conclusions   _____

Section D: Listening Constructively   _____

Section E: Getting to the Essence   _____

Section F: Exploring Disagreement   _____

Next, plot these scores on the Communication Skills Profile Model (Figure 1). Plot your average score for each category on the appropriate line in the pie chart and then join the dots, forming a hexagon. The area within the hexagon indicates your ability to communicate effectively.

Figure 1. The Communication Skills Profile Model.

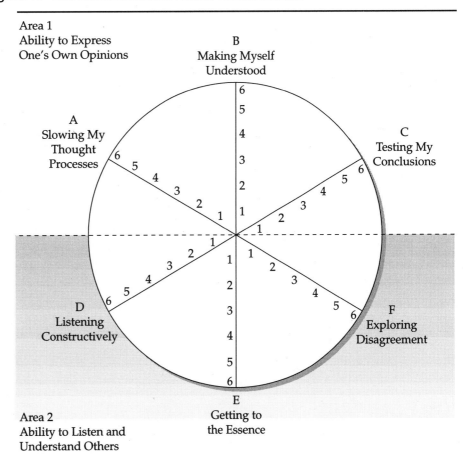

Area 1
Ability to Express
One's Own Opinions

B
Making Myself
Understood

A
Slowing My
Thought
Processes

C
Testing My
Conclusions

D
Listening
Constructively

F
Exploring
Disagreement

E
Getting to
the Essence

Area 2
Ability to Listen and
Understand Others

Consider the following points about the model:

• The more regular the polygon, the higher the balance among the different skills. This does not mean that nothing is to be improved, but that all the different elements are to be considered equally.

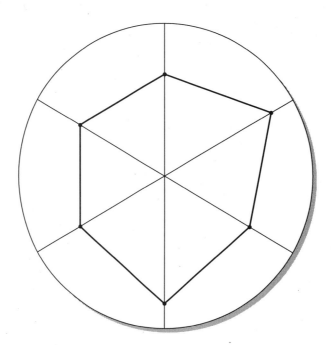

- A small polygon means that gaps are high in all skills; in this case, a plan should be defined so as to stimulate progressive improvements in all directions.

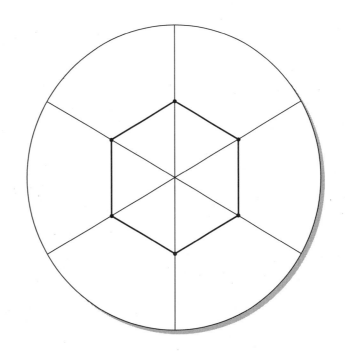

- • Large polygons indicate generally good communication ability.

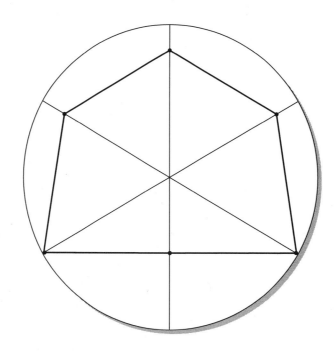

- Polygons with irregular shapes show good communication in some elements, with improvement needed in others. In this case, it is relevant to determine whether or not the skills needing improvement all fall in one of the two main areas, indicating a need to focus attention there.

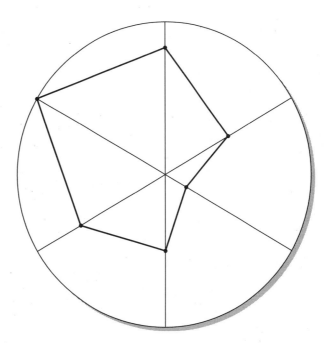

CHAPTER 5

Interpretation and Analysis

Gap Analysis

Gap analysis means comparing the profile from your pie chart with the ideal profile, which is, of course, the largest possible polygon.

It is a good idea to calculate the gap for each individual category and for both of the two major skill areas: *expressing one's own opinions* and *listening and understanding to others*.

The gap for each category can be represented graphically with a bar chart (Figure 2). Each bar represents one of the six skills in the two main areas of communication. Mark a line on each bar representing your score on that skill. The differences between your scores and the ideal score ("6") represent the areas in which you can improve. The bar chart will give you a spot check of whether your weaknesses lie in single categories or in one of the two main areas. Figure 3 is an example of a completed gap analysis.

Figure 2. Individual Gap Analysis Bar Chart.

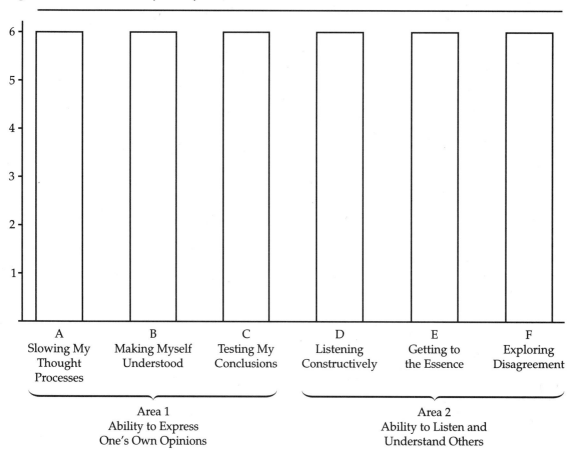

This gap analysis may help you in understanding your profile, because it tells you if the skills to develop belong to a particular area or are distributed in both areas. In the case that your profile shows clearly high values in one of the two areas and low values in the other, you will have to start working on those skills that are not much developed.

A good example of this case would be a profile that shows you have high abilities in expressing your opinions (you know how to make yourself understood by your partners and how to test your conclusions) but reduced abilities in listening to and understanding others (you make less effort to listen constructively and do not explore disagreement).

However, if gaps are present with the same intensity in both areas, you should concentrate your energies to improve the specific skills revealed as weaknesses.

Figure 3. Sample Completed Gap Analysis Bar Chart.

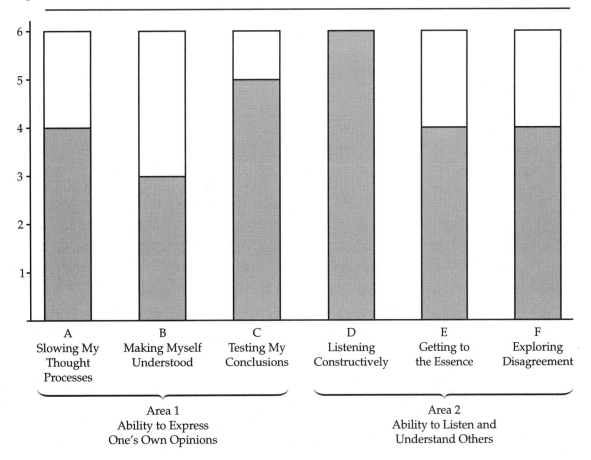

Both areas and all six categories are important. The gap analysis will show you where your weaknesses lie and where you should concentrate your energies if you want to communicate more effectively.

Large gaps in the category of expressing your own opinions could mean that generally you are better at listening than speaking. You have a good overview of the situation but your contributions to discussions are limited. You should realize that what you have to say is important, and you should try to say it clearly and simply, concentrating on improving the categories with the largest gaps.

Large gaps in listening to and understanding others might mean that during meetings you do most of the talking and often interrupt others. Remember that it is important for others to express their own ideas and that by listening to them you have nothing to lose and everything to gain. Perhaps you overlooked something that can only come to light if you let people explain fully.

Concentrate on the categories in which the gap is largest. The following sections describe each category in turn.

Slowing Our Thought Processes

Thought is an extremely rapid process; the human mind is capable of receiving, evaluating, interpreting, and classifying thousands of stimuli simultaneously. Most of this activity takes place unconsciously.

We are generally aware of the results of this communication, not the process. But if we want to make our thought processes understandable to others, we have to be able to explain each of these phases. People want to hear not only our conclusions but also how we reached them.

Slowing our thought processes basically means becoming conscious of each phase and the logical connections between phases. Of course, only when we are aware of them can we explain them to others. This is also a method of checking leaps of logic—steps in the process that are not entirely logical—and modifying our views accordingly, on the basis of what we have overlooked.

If your hexagon shows room for growth in this category, consider that you may be unable to explain your thought processes clearly and exhaustively because you are not fully conscious of them. People may take your views to be more the result of intuition than reasoning. This makes people skeptical about your conclusions and unable to support them fully. Some may even suspect that you are hiding something—some data that do not fit in with your conclusions or some information you do not want to share.

You should try to slow your thought processes down in order to analyze each phase. A good exercise would be to write down each phase and then look at the phases in order to see if you have overlooked any alternatives. Write down the reasons you have discarded certain options. The most important part of the exercise is to write down the deep underlying convictions that guided your thinking. This will help you to explain your point of view more fully and to improve the effectiveness of your communication skills.

Making Ourselves Understood

If we all speak the same language, what is the problem? Sharing one language is no guarantee of understanding. Words have different shades of meaning, and some may mean nothing at all to other people.

Our use of technical terms, jargon, or departmental language with an outsider may make what we say difficult to follow. It is important to use the vocabulary, expressions, and metaphors that the listener readily understands. The same is true of the data we present to support our opinions.

Checking that our language is appropriate is one of the most important ways of making ourselves understood. In addition, it is a mark of respect that generally raises our partner's attention span and interest in what we are saying.

If you need to improve your ability to make yourself understood, you may have a wealth of experience and knowledge that few others possess. Sometimes you may overlook the fact that others may not understand the terminology you use. This forces people through mental hoops in order to follow your reasoning, and if they do not consider the subject of vital importance, you may lose their attention. If people don't grasp what you are saying, they stop listening.

You should try to identify the experiences you have in common with your partner and use the vocabulary of that field of experience. Use words, images, and metaphors that are close to your partner's world. Keep your language, syntax, and grammar simple. Above all, check that your partner is following you. Ask that person to put what you have said into his or her own words. Remember that a good communicator is responsible for the effectiveness of what he or she says and does not blame a lack of understanding on the partner.

Testing Conclusions

Expressing doubts and reservations about our own conclusions is not a sign of weakness but of intelligence. Encouraging others to ask questions does not weaken our position; rather it strengthens the position of the group as a whole.

Successful groups do not try to hide the weakness of a certain conclusion or the lack of real evidence or any other kind of shortcoming. The more these problems come out, the better the conclusions will be.

Clearly this means discussing points on their merits rather than pushing a particular line. Group members are not in competition with one another to see who has the best solution to offer or whose point of view is the most likely one to come up with answers. The purpose of communication and dialogue is to reach solutions that no single member of the group could have reached on his or her own.

If you need to improve in the category of testing your conclusions, you may have all the data at your fingertips. You have thought about them and come to the right conclusion. You are convinced, but you have not felt it necessary to convince others.

You should be more open to doubt—maybe you have overlooked something. Perhaps someone else's point of view is equally valid, or it could be that others could help you to improve on the solution you are putting forward.

Try to let others in on the reasoning behind your conclusions, encouraging them to ask questions and seek clarification. Questions are not personal attacks. If you have any doubts, express them and ask the group to help you clear them up. Ask the group members if they have any other information that might shed a light on your conclusions or any steps used in reaching them.

Do not feel that doubts about your conclusions are doubts about you or your professionalism. This will help you to accept criticism and to work with others more constructively.

Listening Constructively

Listening is not the same as hearing someone out. A person who wants to communicate does not want to be faced with a blank show of interest, a nodding head, and a generally neutral face. He or she wants to be understood, and understanding requires effort. This is easier to achieve if we can eliminate the noise in our own heads, the thoughts that distract from the subject at hand. We will also be able to understand our partner better if we pay attention not only to his or her words but also to the way in which the words are said, the tone, and the body language—the vital nonverbal elements of communication.

The real purpose of listening is to get a clear picture of what someone is saying; helping that person to explain his or her thoughts in the clearest possible way. Judgment comes later.

To improve in this important aspect of communication is to enhance your ability to receive a message. It is also the area that is most often neglected or taken for granted. People assume that they understand even if they do not give their full attention to their partner. This assumption is rarely true.

Remember that listening requires a specific act of will. It means freeing your mind of other concerns. It is not easy, but with time and practice excellent results can be achieved.

Try to reformulate what is being said to you in your own words. Only the speaker can tell you whether your listening has been effective. If you do not have time to listen, postpone the conversation until you do have time. That is much better than pretending to pay attention. Your body language would betray your lack of interest.

Getting to the Essence

No matter how clear the message we have received, it is likely that we will want to ask some questions in order to understand fully. Questions are an important part of getting to the essence. We must be careful, however, how we ask them.

No one likes to be interrogated or to feel subjected to a verbal examination. A calm tone of voice, strict adherence to the issues, and an explicit desire to understand all foster communication. Open-ended questions also help our partner to feel relaxed and to answer openly.

To improve in this category, think more as a child thinks. Children are natural, inoffensive questioners. You may have lost this ability to show interest and inquisitiveness, perhaps fearing your partner's reaction or perhaps because you are not interested or inquisitive. Whichever the real cause, by failing to ask questions, you are receiving messages that are incomplete.

Try to ask more questions, because the answers people provide might be important stepping stones to other solutions. Ask questions calmly, explaining the reason you are asking, which is to understand and not to attack your partner. If that person replies defensively, reassure him or her. In this way you will improve your communication skills, and the group as a whole will benefit.

Exploring Disagreements

Disagreements and conflict are some of the most important resources available to any group, provided they are handled properly. Disagreements should never be ignored nor should they be exacerbated. Quite simply they should be investigated in order to understand their cause. Perhaps two people started off with different sets of data, or they have two different interpretations of the same data, or the disagreement is not about the issue at all but about the use of certain terms and expressions.

Whatever the cause, a properly investigated disagreement is a powerful source of learning, uncovering new ideas and putting others to the test. A large number of excellent solutions come to light only after a disagreement.

Of course it is not easy. No one likes to go into difficult or thorny issues. Yet the benefits far outweigh the risks. If you need to improve in this category, it may be that you tend to avoid conflict and hide potential disagreements. When they cannot be avoided, you react emotionally.

The most important thing to learn is that conflict and disagreement are potentially extremely constructive. If handled properly, they can be the source of new ideas and imaginative solutions. If you find yourself in disagreement with someone, say so, calmly, in an even tone of voice. If you see two people who do not agree on something, help them to explore the reason.

The first step is always to discover the cause of the disagreement: make the meanings of words explicit; analyze the data and each step in the reasoning process. Do not change the positive atmosphere of a meeting by challenging people or by being emotional. If things seem to be getting out of hand, take one step back, summarize the points of agreement, or—failing this—allow things to cool off. Remember that there are no winners and losers, only decisions to be made in the most constructive way.

CHAPTER 6

Action Planning

You have identified the weaknesses in your communication skills. Your Action Plan will be built around them.

Instructions: First, answer the following questions.

What are the three categories in which you have the largest gap?

    1.

    2.

    3.

    Are they in the area of expressing or listening?

Why are they important?

    1.

    2.

    3.

What are ways in which these gaps affect your communication/relationships with others?

    1.

    2.

    3.

What are the measures you intend to adopt to improve your communication skills?

    1.

    2.

    3.

Once you have decided what actions you want to put into practice in order to improve your communication and dialogue skills, you will draw up a real action plan, fixing duties and dates. But remember that work does not end here. When you reach the fixed dates or achieve the results you have in view, fill out the Communication Skills Profile again. The new evaluations will probably be different from the previous ones. Gaps may be reduced compared to those pointed out earlier. If so, you should now concentrate your efforts on the weak points you could not consider before, when they were less evident than the others.

The Action Plan

Instructions: Complete the following statements.

In the _____ category,
I will adopt the following measures by the date indicated:

In the _____ category,
I will adopt the following measures by the date indicated:

In the _____ category,
I will adopt the following measures by the date indicated:

CHAPTER 7

Feedback

At this point, it would be valuable to discuss your individual action plan with others whom you know well. Start by sharing your impressions of the categories in which you plan to take action. Ask for the other person's impressions and suggestions for improvement. Test out how realistic your action plans may be, and solicit support for your goals.

CHAPTER 8

Notes for Work Groups

The Communication Skills Profile may be completed individually or by a team. Completing the profile within a team enables the team to monitor both the separate members' and the team's skills, enabling the members to start from a common vantage point. Therefore, an action plan for the work group may be developed together with the individual plans.

The following questions may help in the definition of the action plan:

- What do I need to improve?
- What prevents me from establishing a dialogue with others?
- Which are the restraints that prevent me from behaving in a certain manner?

It is important that respondents acknowledge the factors that make it difficult to put concepts into practice. These factors should be linked either to the person (behaviors, prejudices, and conditional circumstances) or external elements connected with the environment in which the analysis takes place.

For work groups, two levels of action planning are suggested:

1. Planning to work on common actions, where each member is responsible for achieving improvement.

2. Planning to work individually, where each member undertakes the task of eliminating his or her own gaps so as to develop personal communication skills and at the same time stimulate dialogue within the group.

The Communication Skills Profile can also be used as a post-test to assess the progress that individuals and work teams are making to improve their communication skills. The questionnaire can be retaken any time that results are being seen. And if the newly completed profile should point out other gaps (usually less relevant than those already filled), the respondents may decide to make new action plans.